the
HAWAIIAN
BAT

the HAWAIIAN BAT

'Ōpe'ape'a

Marion Coste

Illustrated by Pearl Maxner

Science Advisor
Theresa Cabrera Menard

A Latitude 20 Book

UNIVERSITY OF HAWAI'I PRESS
Honolulu

© 2005 University of Hawai'i Press
All rights reserved
Printed in China

10   09   08   07   06   05   6   5   4   3   2   1

ISBN 0-8248-2797-X

University of Hawai'i Press books are printed on
acid-free paper and meet the guidelines for
permanence and durability of the Council on
Library Resources

Designed by Santos Barbasa Jr.

Printed by the Everbest Printing Company, Ltd., China

To the children of Hawai'i,
who hold the future of the islands
in their hearts and hands

For my dear friend Patty,
who shares my love of
all things wild

Acknowledgments

Marion and Pearl wish to thank all the people who helped them develop this book. Special thanks to Theresa Cabrera Menard, Ph.D., for her patience in explaining scientific concepts and for reading and rereading the text. The author and illustrator also acknowledge the valuable contributions of Gary Anderson, Sierra Club; Barbara French, Bat Conservation International; Sam Gon, Nature Conservancy; Norm and Ann Goody, proprietors of Three Ring Ranch, an exotic animal sanctuary; Jack Jeffries and Bill Doar, wildlife photographers; Carla Kishinami, Bishop Museum; Dr. Ben Okimoto, Honolulu Zoo; Robert Pyle, Bishop Museum; Pat Winters, who rescues bats in California; and Lilinoe Andrews, who helped us discern the appropriate meanings of some Hawaiian words. Marion also appreciates the manuscript review by her Society of Children's Book Writers and Illustrators (SCBWI) critique group: Gerda Turner, Alice Terada, Kathy Ratliffe, and Margaret Tom.

In ancient times, Hawaiians thought the bat's wing, its skin stretched over a frame of slender bones, looked like *pe'a*, the wind-filled sail of the great voyaging canoes. The people watched bats swoop and dart in the evening sky and named them *'Ōpe'ape'a*, flying sails.

1

igh on the trunk of the ironwood tree, the bat turns and turns again. Bright shafts of Hawaiʻi's morning sun cut through the drooping branches. Usually, the bat is deep in sleep by now, but today, she is awake and restless.

The bat rests for a minute, then shifts again. A warm June breeze moves through the trees and ruffles her thick gray fur. As the ironwood branches sway around her, the bat

3

turns sideways, grips the tree trunk tightly with her claws, and pushes her first baby into the world.

The baby bat slips feet first into the furry pouch made by his mother's curled tail. His tiny eyes and ears are still firmly shut. He can neither see nor hear. His feet are strong, though, and he grips his mother's fur. She bends and licks him gently, cleaning the thin silver hairs that cover his back.

A few minutes later, another baby lies squirming in the tail pouch. Both babies nuzzle at their mother's fur until they find her nipples. Then they cling and suck hungrily, one on each side. Mother bat cradles the babies with her wings and licks them clean and dry.

Hanging upside down on the tree trunk, mother bat folds her wings around her newborn pups. Her frosted gray-brown fur blends perfectly with the rough bark of the ironwood, and when she stops moving, she seems to disappear. As summer clouds drift slowly through the afternoon sky, all three bats drop off to sleep.

Later, in the quiet glow of sunset, mother bat stirs. Shifting her wings, she feels the babies nestled in her fur. The ironwoods are deep in shadow.

A scuffling sound below startles mother bat. A rat scratches at the base of the tree, then stands on his hind legs to sniff up the trunk. Fearful for her babies, mother bat pushes away from the tree and glides into the air. The babies tighten their hold on her fur and grasp her nipples with tiny curved teeth. Mother bat is not used to the pups' extra weight, and she drops toward the ground for an anxious moment before her strong wings take over and sweep them all away from danger.

The first stars glimmer in a dark-ening sky as mother bat flies in a wide circle above the trees. She follows a small stream toward the ocean, flying straight and fast. In a moment, she is over the beach, skimming along the trees at the edge of the sand. With a quick turn, she lands in a *hala* tree. Gently, she pushes her babies off, guiding them until they grip the tree trunk side by side.

Leaving the pups hidden in the deep shadows of the *hala* leaves, mother bat flies swiftly out to sea.

The brisk evening breeze, blowing down the mountains, has picked up insects and swept them out across the ocean. They swarm like a living cloud offshore, waiting for the wind to blow them back to land. Mother bat, hungry after her daytime sleep, dives into the middle of the insect cloud.

Mother bat needs more food than usual while she nurses her pups. She is a good hunter, swift and sure. As she flies, she opens her mouth and sends out calls too high for human ears to hear. The calls bounce off objects in the air and come back as echoes to tell her what things are near. Tonight, the echoes tell her moths—her favorite food—are in the air.

Mother bat chooses a moth and closes in. The nearer she gets to her prey, the faster her calls echo back. Mother bat flies up behind the moth and clamps her strong jaws around the moth's soft body. Its head and wings fall into the sea below. Another bat gets too close to her hunting territory, and mother bat chases him away with sharp, angry calls.

For almost an hour mother bat flies over the ocean, feeding on moths, beetles, and flying termites. Because she has just given birth, she tires quickly and returns to shore before the other bats.

She finds her babies still clinging to the *hala* tree and pulls them onto her body to nurse. As they suck, she licks them gently.

Just before the sun comes up, mother bat flies out on one more hunt. This time she stays on shore, searching for insects along the edges of the stream. As the first streaks of sunlight creep across the sky, she gathers up her pups and flies back to her roosting tree. Clasping the ironwood trunk upside down, she tucks her babies

under her wings and goes to sleep.

By the third day, the baby bats' ears are open and they make chirp-ing sounds. Mother bat leaves them hidden in shadows when she goes hunting and returns two or three times during the night to let them nurse. She calls to the pups as she nears their roosting tree, and they chirp in answer. When she lands, they clamber eagerly up her furry body to get milk.

The pups grow fast. Their eyes open when they are 12 days old, and before the month is out, they can fly. They launch them-selves for short flights while their mother is nearby. One night, one of the pups misses his landing and tumbles to the ground. He calls frantically, and mother bat circles overhead, calling back. The pup is in great danger. He is slow and clumsy on the ground, and rats, cats, and mongooses hunt in these woods.

other bat drops down to rescue the frightened pup. She lands
on a low bush and calls to him. He answers, scrabbling awkward-
ly across the ground toward her. Calling repeatedly, mother bat
urges her pup to climb into the bush. Using the sharp claws on his
thumbs, the pup struggles up until he reaches his mother. She lets
him rest a minute, then they both fly to the other pup who waits
overhead, chirping anxiously. When they are safe, the pups snug-
gle in to nurse.

During the next few weeks, the little bats learn how to hunt,
what to eat, where to roost, and how to keep their fur clean and
smooth. By the time they are two months old, they hunt alone and
roost apart from their mother. They no longer need the comfort of
their mother's fur.

By September, the young bats are fully grown. All three
bats have eaten well during the summer. They're sleek and fat.
Sometimes, on these warm fall nights, they join other bats flying
in a small group, males and females together. Once or twice, male
bats come and fly close to mother bat and they mate in the air.
Mother bat will have new babies next June.

The fall weather gets cooler and wetter. An ancient instinct, like a voice deep inside, pulls the male bats and they fly to feeding grounds higher up the mountain. The females stay along the coast through the fall, but then they, too, fly higher. By January, many bats are living in the mountains.

One afternoon, the weather changes. The air grows heavy and still. When the bats wake up at sunset, they find hardly any insects flying. The wind begins to blow, and rain lashes through the air. The wind builds until it bends the trees sideways. Chilled, the bats cover the fronts of their bodies with their furry tail membranes and cling tightly to their roosts.

All night long the wind whistles and trees twist in the winter storm. Day comes, and the wind grows even stronger. Huge branches split and fall to the forest floor. The wind drives torn bits of leaves and splinters of wood through the blinding rain.

All at once, the storm is over. The wind stops and the rain dies away. Clouds turn into wisps and drift across the sky. A pale sun shines. By afternoon, the day is clear and warm, but the storm has left its scars.

Sun sets and darkness spreads quickly across the mangled forest. Mother bat climbs through a maze of broken branches and spirals upward into the sky. Below her, another bat creeps out, then another. The bats fly through the darkness, sending out their silent cries in search of food. They have not eaten in two days.

The bats fly off in different directions to hunt. Mother bat goes higher up the mountain, feeding on anything she can catch: beetles, moths, and termites. She uses her wingtips like hands to grab insects. Reaching down to chew them up, she turns somersaults in the air. She rests for a while in the middle of the night, then hunts again just before dawn. Morning light finds her sleeping in a *māmane* tree.

When spring comes, mother bat flies back down the mountain. She searches for the ironwood trees, but they are gone. Instead, the outline of a new golf course runs along the ocean's edge. Mother bat flies across the golf course and finds a few trees still standing near the beach. She settles into one and rests.

Just after sunset, mother bat rises into the warm May night. Her body is round with new life, and she feels babies moving inside. Out over the ocean she flies to hunt alone. She darts above the water, feeding, then flies back to shore and swoops into a *hala* tree at ocean's edge. Clinging to the bark, she grooms the soft fur along her wings and down her bulging belly. She folds her wings and settles down to rest. As she sleeps, new life stirs within her small, soft body, a promise that nature's cycle will soon begin again.

Information about Bats

Bats: Enemies or Friends?

Through the ages, myths and stories have portrayed bats as evil and dangerous. People usually think about bats with fear and disgust. Yet bats, of all the wild animals, may be our best friends.

Some bats help fruit crops grow. Bats that eat fruit scatter seeds and cause new fruit trees to spring up. Nectar-eating bats carry pollen from plant to plant, like bees. By scattering seeds and pollinating plants, these bats help produce such foods as avocados, bananas, figs, guavas, and mangoes.

Some bats help get rid of insect pests. Seventy percent of all bats are insect-eaters, or insectivores (in-SEK-tih-vorz), who can eat half their weight in insects in a night. This adds up to a lot of insects!

Bats contribute to scientific research. Scientists have studied bat echolocation (the way bats send out calls and listen to echoes) to figure out how to help blind people find their way around. Vampire bats have a chemical in their **saliva** that keeps blood from clotting. Drugs made from this chemical help humans who suffer from stroke or heart disease. Researchers studied bats that can lower their body temperature and slow down their body systems. The scientists then figured out how doctors can lower people's body temperatures to make certain kinds of surgery more successful.

Bats are **sentinels** of the **environment.** They react to changes in air temperature or humidity and are affected by **pesticides** and pollution. If bats are healthy, we know the environment is healthy. If bats begin to sicken and die, it's a sign that something is wrong in the **ecosystem.**

Three Common Myths about Bats

1. All bats carry rabies.

Bats do not fly around looking for people to bite. Bats are shy animals who try to stay away from humans. Also, bats are not rabies *carriers*—that is, they cannot transmit the disease without getting sick themselves. Very few bats (less than 1/2 of 1 percent) actually catch rabies. If people handle bats with rabies, they may get bitten and catch the disease, just as they would if they handled a rabid dog or mongoose. Every year, however, more people are killed by lightning or bee stings than by rabid bats.

2. Bats get caught in your hair.

If you've ever stood outside at sunset in summertime and seen a cloud of tiny flying bugs gather over your head, you can guess why bats will sometimes swoop near. It's the bugs they're after, not your hair! Flying bats are very good at avoiding objects, and they're not about to bump into your head.

3. Vampire bats bite you on the neck and suck out your blood.

Vampire bats only live in Central and South America and they are very small—about as long as your index finger. A full-grown vampire bat weighs about 2 ounces. These little creatures don't stick fangs in people's necks and suck blood. They don't even have fangs, and they would much rather have deer or **peccaries** (PEK-a-rees) as dinner hosts.

When vampire bats feed, they use their sharp front teeth to make shallow cuts in an animal's skin, then they lick the cut. Vampire saliva has a special chemical called an anticoagulant (an-tee-coh-AG-u-lent) that keeps the blood flowing, so the bat can drink as much as it needs—about 2 tablespoonfuls. When the bat leaves, a scab forms and the cut heals.

Bat Facts

One-fourth of all the mammals in the world are bats. There are more than 1,000 different bat species. Bats have been on earth for at least 50 million years. Today, they are found everywhere in the world except the most remote desert or polar areas. Bats range in size from the huge flying foxes of Southeast Asia with six-foot wingspans, to the tiny bumblebee bats of Thailand, which weigh less than a penny. Bats are **nocturnal,** meaning they sleep during daytime. When they rest, they hang upside down.

Bats are so unique, they have their own animal order: Chiroptera (ki-ROP-ter-ah), which means "hand-winged." A bat's wing has four long, skinny fingers and a short, stiff thumb. A bat uses its wing in much the same way you use your hand.

Bats are mammals, which means they have backbones and hair, have their babies live (they don't lay eggs), are **warm-blooded,** and nurse their young. Many people think bats look like flying mice, but mice are **rodents** and bats are **primates.**

Bat Adaptations

Bats have four special abilities that set them apart from other animals.

1. Flight
Bats are the only mammals that fly. They don't glide like flying squirrels but have true, flapping flight. Bats have large chests with

strong muscles that power their wings, and their flexible wrists and fingers make them skillful fliers.

Researchers using slow-motion cameras discovered that bats use their legs as well as their wings when they fly, just as people use their arms and legs when they swim.

2. Echolocation

People used to think bats had poor eyesight because they live in the dark. Most bats actually have very good eyesight, but they don't depend on their eyes to find their way around in the dark. They have a better tool: echolocation, or *biosonar.*

When bats echolocate, they send out calls that bounce off nearby objects, creating an echo. If the echo tells the bat it has found an insect good to eat, the bat closes in. The closer the bat gets to its prey, the faster it sends out sounds. The echolocation of a hunting bat sounds like *putt . . . putt . . . putt . . .* while the sounds of a bat near its prey are so close together they sound like *buzzzzz.*

The ability to fly plus the ability to use echolocation means bats can find food where few other animals can—in the air, in the dark. The night sky is the bats' **niche,** their own special place in the world of nature.

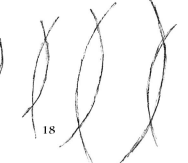

3. Torpor

Bats are warm-blooded animals, which means they must eat to get energy to keep their bodies at a certain temperature. Some bats save energy by lowering their body temperature. Their breathing and heart rates slow down and they seem to be in a deep sleep, a state called **torpor**.

As bats come out of torpor, they are slow-moving and seem sick or even dead. It takes them a few minutes to recover, and they may shiver to raise their body temperature. Some scientists think Hawaiian bats are able to go into torpor when they rest during the day.

4. Hanging reflex

Why don't bats drop out of the trees when they go to sleep? A special reflex tightens the muscles in their legs and feet when they relax, so that they grip their roost firmly even when they're asleep.

Information about the Hawaiian Bat

Scientific name: *Lasiurus cinereus semotus*

Hawaiian name: *ʻōpeʻapeʻa*

The complex little Hawaiian bats are animals of mystery. They are Hawaiʻi's only native land mammals, and some scientists think they may be the rarest bats in the world. Others suspect there are plenty of Hawaiian bats, but we just don't see them. We do know from bones and remains that bats have been in Hawaiʻi for at least 100,000 years. Scientists have a hard time studying Hawaiian bats because the bats live alone, they come out only when it gets dark, and they are very hard to catch. Much of what we *think* we know about Hawaiian bats is based on what we *do* know about their ancestors, continental **hoary** bats.

Hoary bats are strong fliers and famous for wandering far from home. Scientists think that thousands of years ago, a small group of hoary bats living in North or South America got caught in a storm as they were **migrating** and were blown out to sea. The bats continued to fly until they reached the Hawaiian islands, probably landing on the big island of Hawaiʻi.

Description

Some of the Hawaiian bat's hairs have white tips, making its fur look hoary, or "frosted." The Hawaiian bat's wings measure about 13 inches tip to tip, and its body is about 5 inches long (including the tail). It weighs about half an ounce. Females are larger than males. When its wings are wrapped around its body, you can easily hide a Hawaiian bat in your closed hand.

Like all bats, the Hawaiian bat has a short body and slender legs with knees that seem to bend backward. Long, thin finger bones connected by a **membrane** form a wing. Its short thumb has a claw. Soft fur runs along the top of the wings. The Hawaiian bat's tail is connected to its body by a fur-covered membrane that forms a pouch when the bat curls its tail. The Hawaiian bat's feet are long, with strong claws that help it cling. Its neck is very flexible, enabling the bat to look around while it's hanging upside down.

Adult Hawaiian bats are brownish-gray. Young bats are more reddish in color, and newborns have dark stripes down the middle of their backs. A "ruff" of thick fur grows like a collar around the bat's head, making its face seem small. The Hawaiian bat has short, round ears and small, bright black eyes. It is a "simple-nosed" bat, lacking the odd-looking "nose leaf" of many other bats. It has a large mouth with jaws strong enough to crush hard beetle shells.

Hoary bats make two types of calls: **audible** calls, which humans can hear, and **ultrasonic** calls, too high-pitched for human ears. They use audible calls to chase other bats out of hunting areas and to communicate with their pups. They use ultrasonic calls to navigate in the air, avoid obstacles, and catch prey. When hoary bats are disturbed or angry, they hiss like cats.

Hawaiian bats cling upside down to the trunks of trees. When they roost, they are so well **camouflaged,** they seem to disappear, making it hard for **predators** (and bat researchers) to see them.

Habitat

Hawaiian bats live and breed on the islands of Hawai'i and Kaua'i, and they have been seen on Maui, Moloka'i, O'ahu, and Kaho'olawe. Hawaiian bats are solitary animals, preferring to live alone. They usually roost in trees, but researchers have found bats in lava bubbles, in bushes, on fences, on window screens, and even on a car's radio antenna.

Hawaiian bats rest in both **native** and introduced trees and

bushes. They are opportunistic, which means they will use what-ever roost is available.

Hawai'i's bats thrive in the islands' warm temperatures, but they don't seem to mind frosty mornings high in the mountains. They are strong fliers and will fly in light rain, but not when it rains hard. Light wind doesn't bother them.

Hawaiian bats hunt in open areas near the edges of trees, rather than in dense forests. Bats who hunt near the ocean may fly out over the water to feed. People sometimes see bats darting around streetlights at night, and every once in a while, zipping through a car's headlights.

Food

Hawaiian bats eat many different kinds of insects, including beetles, moths, termites, flies, and mosquitoes. Many of the **introduced species** in the Hawaiian bat's diet are pests, such as damp wood termites, mosquitoes, and sugarcane leafhoppers.

Hawaiian bats eat as they fly, catching prey with their mouths or using their wingtips like hands to move flying insects into their mouths. Sometimes, a bat will put a large insect in its tail pouch, then reach down and grab the insect with its mouth. This motion causes the bat to turn a somersault in the air. If the insect is a large moth, the bat

23

chomps off the wings and head and lets them drop to the ground as it eats the soft body.

Bats digest their food very quickly. It only takes about 20 minutes for food to pass through their bodies. Bats have to eat a lot because they use a lot of energy when they fly. A baby bat may eat as much as its whole body weight!

Breeding

Female hoary bats are able to have babies when they are about a year old. The bats mate in the air in early fall, and the male bats probably mate with more than one female. Scientists think female hoary bats can store the males' sperm in their bodies through the winter and delay becoming pregnant until spring. Sometimes, female bats will mate again in the spring.

Female Hawaiian bats give birth in June. They usually have two pups, but the babies are not identical twins. They grow from separate eggs. Every once in a while, a female will have three or four babies. She can nurse all these babies because she has four nipples: two on her breast and two on her abdomen.

Care of the Young

Hoary bat babies cling to their mother's breast and stomach fur with their thumbs and the claws on their feet. They hold onto her nipples with special curved milk teeth. A mother bat will carry her babies away from the roosting place if she feels they are in danger.

When mothers go out hunting, they leave their pups hidden in trees, making sure branches above the babies hide them from anything flying overhead and that there is a clear view of the ground beneath. The babies stay in this spot until their mother returns.

Baby bats are almost hairless when they are born, and their eyes and ears are closed. When the babies are one day old, they begin to make chirping sounds, and by the time they are three days old, their ears are open. The babies' eyes open when they are 11 to 12 days old, and by the time they are four weeks old, they can fly. Young bats stay with their mother for about two more weeks before they go off to live on their own.

Bats must keep their fur in good condition because it affects how well they fly. Smooth, healthy fur is aerodynamic (air-oh-dy-NAM-ik): it has less resistance and helps bats move easily through the air. Hawaiian bats groom their fur often, smoothing it with their tongues, teeth, and claws. Mothers groom their babies, and baby bats begin to groom themselves even before their eyes are open.

Adaptations

When the Hawaiian bat's ancestors arrived in the islands, the habitat they found was far different from the one they had left. Hawai'i had few predators, new kinds of insects, and many unfamiliar trees and bushes. Luckily, the temperature and humidity of the islands was so much like the hoary bats' old habitat that they were able to adapt and survive. Today's Hawaiian bat is about 40% smaller than a North American hoary bat. Its mouth is larger, and its wings are longer in relation to its body size. The bat's small body and long wings enable it to fly easily in small spaces.

Predators and Defense

Owls and other birds may chase bats in the air, and feral cats and rats can climb trees to prey on sleeping bats or babies waiting for their mothers to return. Mongooses, dogs, cats, and rats may pounce on bats unlucky enough to fall to the ground.

When they are threatened, Hawaiian bats hiss and show their teeth. If they are on the ground, they may jump at their attacker. They depend on camouflage to hide them during daylight hours. In the air, Hawaiian bats can turn and dive quickly to get away from predators.

Population

Hawaiian bats have been on the **endangered species** list since 1970, but no one knows how many live in the islands. They are rarely seen and hardly ever cluster in groups or fly in populated areas. Even though scientists don't have exact numbers, they suspect the bat population of Hawai'i is smaller than it once was. On the island of O'ahu, for instance, a scientist in 1816 wrote that the air was "filled with bats" just west of Pearl Harbor. Today, the only bats seen on O'ahu are probably "visitors" who have flown over from Kaua'i, Maui, or Hawai'i, usually in early summer.

Other Bats in Hawai'i

In the distant past, another species of bat came to Hawai'i, but it disappeared, leaving only its bones behind. Scientists think it was related to the red bat, a common North American bat.

Other species of bats were brought to Hawai'i at different times, but none survived. Experiments with Asiatic pipistrelle (PIP-is-trel) and Brazilian free-tailed bats in the late 1800s failed because the people who brought the bats to Hawai'i didn't realize few bat species can adapt to new habitats.

Human Impact

Hawaiian bats depend on trees to live and raise their young. As forests are cut down to make room for hotels, housing developments, golf courses, and shopping centers, bats lose their roosts. Loggers who cut down trees in June and July, when bat pups can't yet fly, may kill a whole generation of bats.

As more people bring new animals and plants to the islands, the balance of nature changes. Bats have had to adapt by finding different kinds of insects to eat and different trees in which to roost. Introduced animals such as rats, feral cats, and birds may prey on young bats.

Toxic chemicals used in fertilizer and pesticides not only kill weeds and insects, but also bats. Bats die if they come into direct contact with these chemicals, or if they eat insects that have been sprayed.

Recovery

Scientists are trying to figure out how to help Hawaiian bats survive. Unfortunately, scientists can't protect bats until they know where the creatures live, what they eat, and what they need in their habitats. Getting this information is difficult because Hawaiian bats are so hard to find.

New technology may help scientists find the bats and figure out how many there are. Perhaps an ultralight radio tag can be fastened safely to a bat to track its movements by satellite. Infrared devices can help researchers see bats in the dark. Maybe someone will think of completely new ways to study bats.

To Learn More about All Kinds of Bats

Bat Conservation International (BCI), PO Box 162603, Austin, TX 78716, is a nonprofit organization that educates the public about the importance of bats, advances scientific knowledge about bats and the ecosystems that rely on them, and preserves critical bat habitats in ways that benefit both people and bats. You can visit their Web site at www.batcon.org.

Glossary

adaptation — change in an animal's body structure or behavior that enables it to survive

audible — within human hearing ranges

camouflage — the color (and sometimes behavior) of an animal that enables it to blend into its surroundings

ecosystem — the interaction of all living and nonliving things that exist together in a certain environment

endangered species — animals or plants that may become extinct

environment — all the surroundings that affect the development of living things

habitat — the area in which an animal lives and can find all it needs to survive

hala — a tree with long, narrow spine-edged leaves and a fruit that looks like pineapple

hoary — white-tipped, frosted

introduced species — animals brought to a location from another place by humans

ironwood — an evergreen tree with rough bark and long, drooping branches

māmane (mah-MAH-nee) — a native Hawaiian tree with narrow leaves and yellow flowers

membrane — a thin, flexible skin-like material

migrating — a group's moving from one place to another, usually at a change in season

myth — an unscientific story, theory, or belief

native — belonging to or found naturally in a certain location

niche (nitch) — the specific place of an organism within its habitat

nocturnal — active at night

peccaries — wild pig-like animals

pesticide — a chemical used to kill weeds and harmful animals

predator — an animal that hunts and eats other animals

primates — animals that have flexible hands and feet, such as apes, lemurs, and humans

rabies — a disease of the central nervous system. Also called hydrophobia

reflex — an automatic muscle action

rodent — a gnawing or nibbling animal, such as a rat, mouse, squirrel, or beaver

saliva — the watery fluid in the mouth that helps digest food

sentinel — someone who guards and warns of danger

torpor — a deep state of inactivity during which body systems are slowed down

toxic — poisonous

ultrasonic — describing a sound pitched too high for human ears to hear

warm-blooded — having a body temperature different from surrounding air temperature

About the Author

Marion Coste, a graduate of Connecticut College, has been an elementary teacher, college instructor, and museum director. Growing up in coastal New Jersey, Marion loved to learn about how different animals live in the wild. She was introduced to the fascinating and fragile world of native Hawaiian wildlife when she worked at Bishop Museum in Honolulu.

Marion is the author of three other books about Hawaiian native species: *Nēnē* (Hawaiian goose), *Honu* (Hawaiian green sea turtle), and *Kōlea* (Pacific golden plover). She has also written *Wild Beach,* a book about a barrier island beach in South Carolina, and *Finding Joy,* the story of the adoption of a Chinese baby girl.

Marion was awarded the Anna Cross Giblin nonfiction grant from the Society of Children's Book Writers and Illustrators in 1991 and received the 1999 *Ka Palapala Poʻokela* Award for excellence in children's literature for *Kōlea.*

About the Illustrator

Pearl Maxner grew up in the Sierra foothills where hiking, bird watching, and her love for nature formed a foundation for her expression as a musician, artist, photographer, and writer. She has worked as a fire lookout and volunteered in both state and national parks in California and Hawaiʻi. Pearl is a graduate of Fresno Pacific College and is a tenured elementary school teacher in Hawaiʻi. She presently resides with her husband Jay on a remote farm on the Big Island of Hawaiʻi. She has three precious children.